Christmas Crafts

Inspired by the traditions of Scandinavia

BONNIER
BOOKS

Christmas Crafts

BONNIER BOOKS

Bonnier Books
Appledram Barns
Birdham Road
Chichester
PO20 7EQ
First published in English
by Bonnier Books, 2007
Copyright © 2006 Bonnier Publications A/S
ISBN: 978-905825-33-2
Bonnier Books website
www.bonnierbooks.co.uk

Contents

Welcome

Christmas is coming, a season steeped in tradition.

With all its different tastes, smells and beautiful things to look at, Christmas is a real treat for the senses.

Feel free to use our ideas, copying them to the letter, or simply as a source of inspiration for something completely different. There are Advent wreaths, Advent calendars, decorations, table decorations, flowers, decorated Christmas trees, delicious things to eat, displays for the home and garden, and things for children, big and small, to make. The templates at the back of the book will help.

Christmas is the time to indulge your creative side – and, just as everyone sings as they dance around the Christmas tree, everyone should also have a go at making Christmas decorations. Do whatever is fun for you, there are no hard and fast rules. And the best loved Christmas decorations are often those which are a little rough around the edges.

Welcome to a lovely Christmas season full of spruce, glitter and joy!

Advent wreaths and flowers

Christmas decorations and Advent wreaths come in all shapes and sizes. Here we have tried something new in Advent wreaths without the greenery, where the four candles are the main elements, and the decorations are based around simple white flowers. Despite the clean look, they fill the entire home with a lovely Christmas feel. We end the chapter with easy ideas with fruit and flowers.

The Legend of the Christmas Rose

tells the story of how the Christmas rose came to bloom in December when all other plants wither away.

"But when Abbot Hans was being taken back to Öved, those who were dealing with the deadman, saw that his hand was tightly gripped around something that he must have taken hold of at the moment of his death. When, finally, they managed to prise open the hand, they saw that he had been clutching a couple of white tubers that he had picked up from among the moss and leaves. And when the lay brother, who had followed Abbot Hans, saw these tubers, he took them and planted them in Abbot Hans' herb garden.

He waited and watched all year to see if they would bloom, but he waited in vain through spring and summer and autumn. When winter came, and all the leaves and flowers were dead, he gave up waiting. But on Christmas Eve, the memory of Abbot Hans was so strong that the brother went out into the herb garden to think about him. And as he went past the place where he had buried the bare tubers in the earth, he saw that vigorous stems had sprouted from them, and that on these stems were beautiful flowers with silver white petals.

He called together all of the monks of Öved, and when they saw this plant bloom on Christmas Eve, when all the other flowers were dead, it became clear to them that it really had been taken by Abbot Hans from the Christmas garden in Gönge Forest. But the lay brother said to the monks that, since a miracle had taken place, they should send some of the flowers to Bishop Absalon."

Extract from The Legend of the Christmas Rose by Selma Lagerlöf.

Christmas Countdown

Should this year's wreath be spruce, steel wire or just four simple candles? There are many options, but it needn't take long to find or make up your wreath. It might be an idea to think a bit differently this year and try something completely new. The most important thing is for you to set aside a quiet moment and enjoy an hour's creative activity by flickering candlelight.

Pillar candles with garland

Four white pillar candles symbolising the four Sundays of Advent. Arrange the candles within a simple wreath made of fencing wire. Allow the wire to overlap slightly and wind thin wire around the join. Twist a metal garland around the steel wire wreath and decorate with small fabric flowers. It's easiest to glue them in place with a glue gun.

With prisms and sequins

Decorate a ready-made steel wreath with glass beads, Christmas baubles, sequins, prisms and flowers.

Attach the items with thin silver wire which is available in all good crafts shops.

Place four traditional candle holders and candles on the wreath.

For the children

The candles are rechargeable and the wreath is plastic, ideal for a child's room. A natural spruce wreath could, of course, be used instead. Decorate with mushrooms and ribbon (available from craft shops) and glue on fabric roses.

Loose numbers

The Advent candle is a thick pillar candle and the numbers are from card. Using the templates, draw the numbers on card, then cut them out. Pour glitter onto a plate. Apply glue to the numbers then dip in the glitter. Punch a hole in the top of the number, make a small tie using a bead, a sequin and silver thread, and attach the numbers with a pin.

Willow wreath

Weave a wreath from pre-soaked thick willow twigs, or buy a ready-made wreath. Wind beaded silver wire (available from craft shops) around the wreath in a criss-cross fashion. Place the candles in the middle. Decorate with silver wax angels which are available from specialist candle shops at Christmas.

Thin silver wreath

Shape fencing wire into the form of a wreath, allowing the two ends to overlap slightly. Wind thin wire around the overlapped section to fasten the wreath.

Wind silver twisel around the wreath and tie on Christm ristmas figures, or use ribbons to hang the wreath from the ceiling.

Sweet centrepiece

For most families the four
Sundays of Advent are a time
for togetherness, a time to
enjoy cakes and sweets while
the candles burn down. This
tiered cake stand represents
this time, with space for the
cakes and sweets and four
candles clipped to the edge
of the plates. Add a touch
of decoration: some small
Christmas baubles, a string of
beads and maybe a few prisms.

Advent vase

Fill the bottom of a vase with sugar and stick four long taper candles into the sugar. Wind a string light with leaves around the vase, embellish with a wreath of beads, flowers or whatever you can find. The string light and flower wreath should hang from a hook on the edge of the vase. The hook can be fashioned out of thick wire (thick iron wire in ready-measured pieces is available from craft shops).

Winter white flowers

Flowers in the home are an integral part of the festive decorations. We show you how to make the most of your flowers in simple, decorative displays. Choose flowers in a colour that complements your Christmas home. Here we have ideas using white flowers.

Daffodils in attractive sandstone pots adorned with a zinc crucifix. The bulbs are covered with white reindeer moss, and a small Christmas candle sits on the edge of the pot. It always works well to have two identical elements in a display – here the pots are placed together on a decorative tray.

The forest is also clothed in winter white.

Stems from the cotton plant, with their cotton snowballs, are paired with long-stemmed, white roses. As an extra decorative touch, glass crystals are hung from the branches, held in place with a small piece of wire. Cotton branches may be ordered from flower shops.

The heads are cut off a white poinsettia and placed in a dish of water with floating candles. Small sprigs of spruce add a touch of green to the decoration. Sprinkle a little silver glitter over the flower heads and candles. Complete the look with a reindeer antler or use a tactile piece of wood instead.

Winter white flowers

Amaryllis is also known as hippeastrum. It is a plant with a large bulb which originates from Peru. The amaryllis flowers once a year, during the winter, when it produces up to two stalks per bulb. Each stalk bears 4-6 large flower heads. The plant should be kept in a light position and be watered sparingly. There are many different varieties in shades of white, red, two-tone and yellow.

The poinsettia originates from Mexico where it also grows as a large tree, reaching up to 4-5 metres (13-15 ft) in height. Cultivated in greenhouses in this country, the poinsettia comes in pink, red, salmon and white, and every year new varieties are added to the range. It is an extremely long-lasting plant which can bloom right up until May.
It can also be used as cut flowers, but they don't keep for long.

The tazetta belongs to the narcissus family, along with the daffodil and white narcissus. It is a bulbous plant with white flowers that grow best in well-drained loamy soil in partial shade. In the wild, the tazetta flowers in the spring, when it produces offset bulbs which double the number of flowers the following year. It can be forced for sale in December.

The rose is a root plant which favours loamy soil, in a sunny position. The rose should be pruned every spring and flowers from early summer until long into the autumn, depending on the type.

The hyacinth is one of the most fragrant bulbous plants. The plant comes in a wide range of colours in shades of white, yellow, blue, pink and red. It blooms naturally in the spring, but can be forced for sale in November.

Long-stemmed amaryllis flowers each in a vase of its own. The stems have been carefully wrapped in white reindeer moss, held in place by a small piece of raffia, tied into a knot. Hanging behind is a large, dried larch branch. Simple, yet very effective.

Cut hyacinths are placed in water in a beautiful glazed tureen together with dried larch branches and cones. If you find it difficult to get the hyacinths to stand up by themselves, fill the tureen with moistened oasis and push the flowers into it.

Simple decorative ideas

Christmas in an instant - the easy way! It's amazing what a little sprig of spruce and a sprinkling of gold glitter can do, when you know what you're doing. We have put together five ideas, ready for you to copy.

Hyacinths provide a fantastic injection of colour in dark times. Buy a mixed bunch and place them individually in glass vases. Change the water daily. Or use different co ured roses.

Large candles arranged in identical glasses half full of fresh cranberries. Tie ribbons around the glasses in colours to match your Christmas decorations. Take the candles out occasionally to shake the berries to prevent those at the bottom from rotting.

Pomegranates are available (to order) from flower shops at Christmas. Give a quick spray of, ideally, gold glitter spray (outside) and arrange with a sprig of holly.

Christmas rose centrepiece
The earth that the Christmas rose is growing in is covered in white reindeer moss. Decorate with some silver baubles and sprinkle with silver glitter.

Roses, Christmas style
Lightly spray the roses with clear varnish and sprinkle with glitter – a lovely, subtle decoration. Float the roses in small glasses together with a sprig of spruce. The water level should be the same in all glasses.

Hanging decorations with roses or juniper berries
Use 50 cm (15 ins) black card wire. Start approx. 5 cm (2 ins) into the wire, so that there is enough wire for a small hook for the pig. Push juniper berries or dried rose heads onto the wire until the wreath measures 10-12 cm (4-5 ins) in diameter. Twist the wire a couple of times. Allow one end to hang down into the wreath and use the remainder of the wire for a hanging loop. Glue two pieces of gift wrap together so that there is pattern on both sides. Trace the pig motif from the template pages, transfer to the paper, cut it out and hang the pig in the wreath. Embellish the rose wreath with a star anise seed pod.

Christmas scents

Sweet, spicy smells are a big part of Christmas and spices are an easy material to work with. Spice decorations can be lain on the side or hung. Here we have bound garlands, made cards and hanging decorations, and sewn scent bags, all of which smell wonderful - a Christmas delight!

Scent bags Cut out two 15 x 15 cm (6 x 6 in) organza squares. Trace the heart and stocking pattern from the template pages and pin to the fabric. Machine around the pattern, leaving an opening for the filling. Cut approx. 1 cm (1/2 in) from the stitching with pinking shears. Fill the bag with cinnamon, star anise, cloves and roses and sew up the opening on the machine. Cut 25 cm (10 in) wire to make a hanging loop. Push the wire through the organza, attach the sequin, and shape the end of the hanging loop into a star.

Scented Christmas card Fold a 22 x 20 cm (9 x 8 in) piece of watermark paper, making it 11 cm (4 1/2 in) wide. Trace the star or pig pattern from the template pages and then onto a plastic sleeve. Cut out the pattern with a craft knife. Place the plastic pocket on the card so that the motifs fit. Spread glue over the paper through the holes in the template and sprinkle cardamom, cinnamon or glitter in the wet glue. Cut out a figure in wallpaper/gift wrap and glue it to the card. You could also outline the figure in glue and sprinkle spices onto the line of glue. Draw with a little silver glitter glue on the card.

Cinnamon garland Glue two sheets of gift wrap or wallpaper (approx. 25 x 25 cm (10 x 10 in)) together. Trace the reindeer motif from the template pages and transfer to the paper. Cut out five reindeer. Wind and thread the different spices onto 2.5 m (8 1/2 ft) black card wire, attaching a reindeer here and there. Decorate the ends of the cinnamon sticks with silver glitter.

The joy of expectation

Secrets, small white lies, rustling paper, curly gift ribbon, the
countdown, small surprises, handwritten Christmas greetings.
Yes, Christmas is a time of excitement when you pull out the stops
and all the tricks come into play, when surprising and pleasing
family and friends.
This chapter shows you how to make Advent calendars,
wrap your gifts and make personal Christmas cards.

And sister Kate she sews and sews,

As Christmas money quickly goes
She shakes her money-box.
For Dad a pipe-string she has got,
And then to keep old Granny hot,
She's knitting her bedsocks.

For me she's making something too,
And I into the hall must go,
When she begins to knit.
It's jolly cold out in the hall,
But when I play there with my ball
I do not notice it.

Before I for my walk was sent,
Into the baker's shop we went,
There stood the man that bakes.
And he wrote down what Reny said —
For Christmas Day, besides the bread,
Two 'normous Christmas cakes.

If it was Christmas, Oh what fun,
It can't take long for it to come,
Oh no, don't tell me that,
For when I from my window look,
Close to the window on a hook,
A goose hangs, nice and fat.

*Extract from Peter's Christmas by Johan Krohn
written in 1863, translated by Hugh F. Pooley.*

Calendars and gifts

The build-up to Christmas can seem endless to children – how do you make it slightly more bearable for them? A small gift in the Advent calendar, every day, throughout December, helps a little. Be inspired and take a new approach to making the Advent calendar and Christmas wrappings for both children and adults this year.

Parcels in bags

A sweet bag can certainly be used as gift wrap if it's nice and clean. The gift tag is written on hologram paper, available from craft shops, and the bag has been closed with a wide velour ribbon, threaded through the top of the rolled up bag – decorate with a small glass bead or a brooch.

The gift in the middle is wrapped in pink tissue paper, wound around with thick brown wool. Glue around the edges of the luggage label and sprinkle with glitter. Decorate with small silk flowers, which are either held in place under the wool or attached with a glue gun.

The gift on the right has been wrapped in transparent paper with a checkerboard design, so that the paper forms a bag. (Similar paper is available from shops selling drawing materials). The bag is tied together at the top with chiffon ribbon. The gift tag is a luggage label with a Biblical motif stuck on it. Finish off with a small silk flower.

Gift tag

Cut a card out of thick paper or card, approx. 6 x 10 cm (2½ x 4 ins). Spread glue around the edges and sprinkle plenty of glitter over it while the glue is wet. This gives a lovely effect, but the whole house does end up full of glitter! You can avoid this by using a tube of glitter glue instead, but the effect is not nearly as good. As an alternative to the white card, you could use the old-fashioned luggage labels in brown card.

Gift wrap from the kitchen

Greaseproof paper and wide elastic bands are usually to be found in the kitchen drawer, and the width of the roll is ideal for smaller gifts. A yellow post it-note functions as a gift tag and the decoration is a small bunch of herbs. Fun, untraditional and cheap!

Felt Christmas stockings

You will need:

0.5 m (18 ins) dark red felt, 1 m (39 in) pompom ribbon, 0.4 m (16 in) felt heart ribbon, red wool, pinking shears and double-sided sticky tape.

Trace the pattern from the template pages. Fold the felt in two, and cut out a stocking around the pattern, leaving a 0.5 cm (1/4 in) seam allowance. Pin around the edges – leaving a 10 cm (4 in) gap from the top on both sides. Glue the ribbons onto the reverse side of the stocking, and stitch them in place (this section will fold down to form a cuff on the outside). Make a strap out of the last pompom ribbon by cutting the pompoms off and attach strap to the inside seam.

Pin together the last 10 cm (4 in) and sew together the sides and base, 1 cm (1/2 in) from the edge. Cut with pinking shears, 0.5 cm (1/4 in) from the seam and along the top edge. Fold over the cuff, so that the ribbons are visible. Iron the stocking on a low temperature setting. Roughly stitch around the edge and in between the ribbons on the foldover cuff with red wool.

A large, exciting parcel

The gift is wrapped in lovely gift wrap, but it's the gift tag that makes it so irresistable to children. Almost no matter how small you are, you can read your name, clearly written all the way around the tag. The tag is made from a piece of red transparent paper, A4 size. Glue a smaller piece of glittery gift wrap on top and attach a sheet of scrap pictures, using a stapler – attach a star sequin in each corner. Write the child's name several times around the edge of the tag with a relief liner pen. Tie silver ribbon with red rickrack trim around the parcel.

Presents by the boxload

You may be given ready-made gift boxes, both round and square, at department stores. Generally speaking, with these it's easy enough to attach a nice ribbon and a small, fun thing to the parcel. It would almost be a shame to wrap up a new cake tin – why not use it as an extra gift and fill it with homemade Christmas biscuits or cookies. Attach a sample to the ribbon.

Paper stocking Advent calendar

You will need:

Gift wrap, a sewing maching, a glue stick, metal foil in different colours, permanent marker pen and pinking shears. Plus card for the template.

The drawing of the pattern:

Trace the stocking pattern, from the template pages, onto card and cut the template out. There are three sizes of stocking to choose between, and the leg can be shortened or lengthened, widened or made narrower, so that it is the right size for the parcel. Lay the gift wrap back to back and draw around the template. Cut the stocking out.

Sewing instructions:

Stitch 1 cm (1/2in) from the edge on the machine's longest stitch length setting. Start by attaching and sewing together along the leg, around the foot and back up the leg on the other side. Place the gift inside the stocking as you go along, and finish off by sewing the stocking together at the top.

Finish:

Cut off the excess paper around the seam with the pinking shears. Draw around a small glass on the metal foil, and cut the circles out with pinking shears. Write the number in the middle and glue the number onto the stocking leg.

Advent calendars hanging on the line

There are countless fun ways that the children's Advent calendars can be presented. In stockings, on stitched Advent calendars, or hung out on a line in the child's bedroom. The only requirement is that the gifts are not so heavy that they risk falling down during the night! Wrap the gifts in a fun way and hang them on a line using clothes pegs, together with a selection of the child's own drawings.

Paper stocking calendar

It's not an insurmountable task to make 24 stockings, when they're sewn out of paper! The size of the stocking is adapted to the size of the gift and can be sewn together in no time. To open the stocking, the child should tear open the stitching at the top. Wait for the smiles.

Gifts in black and white

Christmas presents are usually wrapped in brightly coloured paper, but this year we have also gone for a black and white look. Tear black and white photos out of magazines, or print out family photos in black and white. Glue the photo onto a white box and tie a piece of silver tinsel around as gift ribbon. We used a cardboard drum as a gift tag.

Roasting bag parcels

Roasting bags are made out of bright clear cellophane. Try using them as novel gift bags, but conceal the gifts first in another wrapping paper. We tore pages out of a magazine, taped them together and used them as wrapping paper. The gift tag is cut into a triangle to form a Christmas tree shape – Cut out three layers and tie them together with a snippet of gift ribbon.

Corrugated card and tissue paper parcels

Finely corrugated card is sold in craft shops, and is good for concealing gifts which would otherwise give themselves away due to their shape. Hold the roll together with narrow bands of black card, glued tightly around the roll. Write the name on a narrow black strip of card with a silver pen.

Tissue paper never fails! First wrap the gift in white paper and then in black to form a bag shape. Tightly tie the parcel with a leather lace. Glue small paper wafers to the lace and write the name of the recipient on the circles.

The white parcel has been embellished with a black velour ribbon. Write who the gift is for on a card circle, in gold pen.

33

Great card ideas

A Christmas greeting should be personal. A homemade Christmas card tells the recipient that a lot of care and thought has gone into it. These cards are fun to make – two are easy, the others require a little more work but are well worth it!

Card with winter twigs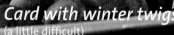
(a little difficult)

You will need: 21 x 20 cm (8¹/2 x 8 in) thick, handmade 320 g paper, silver glitter glue, a darning needle, parchment and hobby glue (all materials available from craft shops).

Score along the middle of the paper with the needle, using a ruler, and fold in two to make a 10.5 x 20 cm (4¹/2 x 8 in) card.

Trace the motif, from the template pages, onto the parchment in pencil. Lay the paper face down on the front of the card, and trace along the lines with a sharp pencil so that the pattern is embossed. Trace over the marked lines with glitter glue. Cut out six leaves and pinch them together along the middle. Glue them onto the silver branches.

Star card (easy)

You will need: 14.5 x 14.5 cm (5³/4 x 5³/4 in) natural coloured card, handmade tissue paper with silk thread, 15 x 15 cm (6 x 6 in) white card, wallpaper paste, a flat brush and double-sided sticky tape.

Tear five oblong pieces of tissue paper that come to a point at each end. The pieces need to fit onto the card. Glue them on top of each other, one-by-one, with the brush and wallpaper paste, onto the natural-coloured card to form a star shape.

Allow the paste to dry and then stick the star onto the white card with double-sided sticky tape.

Stitched star card
(a little difficult)

You will need: 15 x 30 cm (6 x 12 in) white Canson paper, 10.5 x 10.5 cm

(4¹/₄ x 4¹/₄ in) ochre-coloured Canson paper, 9 x 9 cm (3¹/₂ x 3¹/₂ in) white Mulberry paper with embossed pattern, cream handmade textured paper, silver thread, ornament stamp and gold stamping powder, double-sided sticky tape, a ruler, darning needle and pinking shears (all materials available from craft shops).

Trace the star shape, from the template pages, and make a card template. Draw around the template onto the cream textured paper and cut out. Sew the star from point to point with the silver thread on the sewing machine.

Cut around the edges of the white Mulberry paper with the pinking shears. Stick the star on with the double-sided sticky tape. Stick the paper onto the ochre-coloured Canson paper. Stamp a pattern over the entire sheet of paper. Score a fold line with the darning needle using a ruler, and fold in two to create a
15 x 15 cm (6 x 6 in) card. Stick the star on with the double-sided sticky tape.

Glitter circle card (easy)

You will need: 15 x 30 cm (6 x 12 in) cream handmade 320 g paper, silver glitter glue, silver foil, a hole punch, a ruler, darning needle and compass.

Score down the centre of the paper with the needle, using a ruler, and fold in two to make a 15 x 15 cm (6 x 6 in) card. Draw a circle of 12 cm (4³/₄ in) in diameter.
Trace over the line with the glitter glue and continue to squiggle and spiral round and round inside the circle.
Punch holes in the silver foil with the hole punch, and glue the circles here and there in the glitter circle .

Welcoming Christmas tables

Guests are made to feel really welcome when the host goes to that extra little bit of effort with the decorations and a beautifully laid table. We've had great time cutting and sticking, baking and generally busying ourselves with all the preparations.

This chapter is full of ideas, both big and small, for stunning tables throughout the Christmas season and on the big day itself. Be inspired and make your own Christmas table look fantastic, in the style that best suits you and your family.

I do like this time of year

Christmas will very soon be here,
There's snow upon the ground.
Dad goes to town each day, I'm there,
When he comes back, and don't I stare,
His pockets are so round.

And on his table, Oh I say,
I saw a lovely flag one day,
I can't forget I saw her
With scissors, he the paper clips,
But when I come he always slips
It quick into a drawer.

Already Mor's begun to bake,
The gingerbread and no mistake,
I've tasted it quite hot.
Out of the box quite quietly, lest
I'd know where she was gone, the best
Branch candlesticks she's got.

And Mor sends messages about,
To Charles she whispers to go out
And fetch all sorts of things.
I heard them, and I know I'm right,
This morning it was Christmas lights
And prunes and coloured strings.

From Peter's Christmas by Johan Krohn written in 1863, translated by Hugh F. Pooley.

A table all in white

No Christmas is complete without the colour white. From the whitest
of whites to the more creamy tones, using black as a contrast. There is no greater
contrast than black and white, and it works every time – stylish and dramatic.
Doily cones and fine ribbons soften the look.

A second outing for old tablecloths

It's Christmas so get the white cloths out! Our table features a good, old family heirloom – a tablecloth that has been to a party or two! The contrast between the fine, chalk-white tablecloth and the simple plates and beakers rings the changes.

To mark the occasion we've been through the photos in the house and found some that look really good with the simple table decoration. Perhaps you have some black and white photos that would work well and complete the decoration. Another option is to frame some giftwrap and use it as a wall decoration during the Christmas season – or just for a party in the evening.

Ribbon napkin rings

Have a rummage around your sewing basket for pretty woven ribbons, or buy some that are the right width and colour. If flashes of bright colour are more your style, use multicoloured ribbons – this will give your table a different look entirely.

Fold white linen hemstitched napkins twice, and then roll them up. Cut three ribbons to a length of 35 cm (14 in), bunch them together, and tie them tightly around the rolled napkin.

Cones and table name cards

The large beakers needn't stand empty on the table before being used – fill them with delicious mini treats such as a luxury chocolates or some delicate salted almonds. Roll a paper doily into a cone and glue or clip it together. If there are going to be a lot of you at the party, and table name cards are necessary, write the name directly onto the doily, or write it on an oblong piece of card and pop it in the cone.

Festive colours

A fairytale Christmas table with quirky ideas in patterned pastels, gold and sparkling crystals. Reindeer antlers dangle from the chandelier, and the table name cards are toadstools. The glow of tealights is reflected in a plateful of old Christmas baubles. Hyacinths fight their way out from beneath pointed hats pulled well down around their ears.

Toadstool-shaped table name cards

The toadstool-shaped card is covered in a mix of lovely patterned papers. The guest's name or the menu can then be written on the back. Trace the parts of the toadstool from the template pages onto tissue paper. Glue onto card and cut out. Use the card template to draw around. Draw the toadstool parts onto the different patterned papers and cut them out. Glue the two parts together and write on the back.

Free falling antlers

Add a touch of winter to the chandelier with small, decorative reindeer antlers. Trace the antlers, from the template pages onto tissue paper, glue onto card and cut out. Use the template to draw around. Glue two pieces of patterned paper together back to back. Draw around the antler template on the paper, and cut out. Cut a 20 cm (8 in) long piece of wire, push it through the top of the 'head' and twist the ends of the wire together to form a hanging loop.

Pointed wallpaper hats

Add some green 'guests' in brightly coloured glasses, wearing festive hats, to the well-dressed table. Shake the excess earth off the hyacinth bulb, carefully rinse and immerse into a glass containing water – just the roots, not the bulb. Make small, pointed hats for the hyacinths from different patterned papers and wallpaper. Trace the shape, from the template pages, onto tissue paper, glue onto card and cut out. Use the card template to draw around. Draw the hat on paper and cut it out. Score along the fold line with a needle and stick the hat together – double-sided sticky tape is good for this! Place the hat over the hyacinth.

Simple and exotic

Mix the old with the new, the shiny with the matt, and give Christmas a touch of the exotic, with silver and brown as the main colours. There are no napkins or cloth here, as our rustic table is made from bare wood. You can use a dark cloth to achieve the same look.

Invitation and Christmas card

Kill two birds with one stone and send the invitation to this year's Christmas party on a homemade Christmas card.

Cut out a 15 x 18 cm (6 x 7 in) piece of card and glue on a piece of patterned paper. Cut different lengths of sequin ribbon, patterned ribbon and narrow ribbon so that, when placed together, they form a triangle, a Christmas tree. Start with the widest ribbon at the bottom. It should be 11 cm ($8^{1}/_{4}$ in) wide. Continue upwards, ending with a ribbon that is approx. 2.5 cm (1 in) wide. Glue the ribbons onto the card, and finish off with a gold metal disk and a small bell on the top of the tree.

Decorated matchboxes

Plenty of candles are needed to create a real festive atmosphere, hence the need for small decorative matchboxes that can be put out on the Christmas table.

Glue a piece of patterned paper onto the matchboxes, decorating each box differently. One is decorated with a piece of sequin fabric, cut out and glued onto the box with a narrow ribbon underneath. A second is adorned with two narrow ribbons and a gold thread with a small bell and a gold metal coin on it. The third is decorated with a narrow ribbon all the way around the box. The final touch is a small Christmas bauble and a beaded decoration.

Mini hearts from circles

Use the hearts as table name cards by writing the guest's name on a narrow strip of paper placed inside the heart. The hearts are inside the glasses when the guests sit down to the table. Trace the heart circle, from the template pages, onto tissue paper, glue onto card and cut out. Use the card template to draw around. Each heart consists of two circles, cut out from two types of paper, using the template. Fold each circle in half, place one circle inside the other to form a heart shape and glue them together. Cut out a 0.7 x 12 cm (¹/₄ x 8¹/₄ in) handle, fold it in half and glue it to the heart.

Scented Christmas hearts

When you are doing the Christmas baking, bake more than you need so that some biscuits can be used as decoration. Make the dough (or buy it ready-made in the supermarket) and roll it out. Cut out hearts with different sized cutters, make a hole with a straw so that they can be hung up. Bake the biscuits and leave to cool. Thread ribbons of different widths and patterns through the holes of the baked biscuits and hang them over the Christmas table, in the window or in the doorway.

Christmas trees standing proud

Trees are used as table decorations – here one tree per plate works well.

Trace the pattern parts, from the template pages, onto tissue paper (there are 3 parts to each tree). Glue onto card and cut out. Use the card templates to draw around. Draw the parts onto different coloured papers, and cut them out. Cut a jagged edge along the bottom of each of the parts of the Christmas tree. Stick each part together to form a cone shape (double-sided sticky tape is good). Put the three sections together and glue a button onto the top of the tree.

Add a soft edge to a modern, style, with homemade biscuits hung up with embroidered ribbon, cut out Christmas trees and folded hearts. This simple and understated decoration doesn't take long to make. The hanging biscuits are also effective window decorations when a large group hangs from the top of the window frame.

Freshly baked Christmas spirit

Christmas baking

Everything feels so warm and cosy when the whole house smells of
Christmas baking and homemade definitely tastes best! This chapter
is full of nostalgia, with recipes for Scandinavian Christmas classics
such as klejner (twisted doughnuts), pepper cookies and honey cookies.
Children should also be encouraged to lend a hand in the
kitchen at this time of year, so there are also fun suggestions for
sweets, biscuits and fruits for them to make.

Here in Noisy Village there are three farms, North Farm and Middle Farm and South Farm.

In North Farm live Britta and Anna, in Middle Farm live Lasse and Bosse and me, and in South Farm live Ole and his little sister, Kirsten.

This is what Noisy Village looks like in the winter.

When it's Christmas everything is so lovely, especially here in Noisy Village. Life is good, even for the sparrows, as we put Christmas sheaves up for them. And for the bullfinches too, of course, and for all the other hungry little birds.

And life is good for us kids in Noisy Village, and when it's Christmas, life is even better for us than it is for the sparrows. Now I will tell you how it was for us last Christmas, here in Noisy Village.

Three days before Christmas we baked ginger biscuits. And that is almost as much fun as Christmas Eve itself. It smelt of ginger biscuits all over Noisy Village that day.

"That's a smell I like," said Lasse. He baked nineteen pigs, I baked fourteen and Bosse eleven. We also made hearts and stars out of the ginger biscuit dough.

From Christmas in Noisy Village by Astrid Lindgren.

Cakes for everyone

Some people like them dry and crumbly, others prefer them moist and creamy. Some like them baked and some like them deep-fried. And some like them however they come! Here are eight very different Christmas cake recipes to suit every palette, so there is bound to be at least one that becomes a family favourite.

Cranberry and almond tart

- pre-baked tart case, 22 cm (8^1/$_2$ in) in diam., using ready-made shortcrust pastry (or 250 g (8 oz) flour, 100 g (3^1/$_2$ oz) icing sugar, 125 g (4 oz) butter and 2 egg yolks blended with 2 tbsp. cold water)

Filling:

- 150 g (5 oz) cranberries
- 200 g (7 oz) sugar
- 150 g (5 oz) butter, softened
- 200 g (7 oz) unblanched almonds, ground
- 3 large eggs, beaten

Mix the cranberries with 50 g (2 oz) of the sugar, and cream the remainder 150 g (5^1/$_2$ oz) with the butter. Stir the almonds into the butter mixture and then add the beaten eggs. Mix well and fold in the cranberry mixture. Pour the filling into the pre-baked pastry case, smooth out and bake at 160-170°C (320-340°F) for 35-40 minutes.

Jamaican fruit cake

- 350 g (12 oz) raisins and currants, mixed
- 350 ml (12 floz) dark rum
- 200 ml (7 floz) port
- 175 g (6 oz) butter, softened
- 200 g (7 oz) dark muscovado sugar
- grated peel of 1 orange
- 2 large eggs
- 375 g (13 oz) flour
- 1 tsp. ground cinnamon
- ^{1}/$_2$ tsp. grated nutmeg
- ^{1}/$_2$ tsp. ground allspice
- 2 tsp. baking powder

To decorate:

- 150 g (5 oz) apricot jam
- approx. 500 g (1 lb) raw marzipan
- icing of 1^1/$_2$ egg whites, 350-400 g (12-14 oz) icing sugar and 1 tsp. liquid glycerine (from chemists and baking supply shops)

Soak the currants and raisins in the rum and port for 1-2 weeks. Stir the mixture. Mix the butter with the sugar and orange peel, add the egg, a little flour, the spices and the fruit puree. Mix the remainder of the flour with the baking powder and fold into the dough. Pour into a lined, greased spring-form (diam. 22-24 cm (8^1/$_2$ -9^1/$_2$ in)) and bake for approx. 75 minutes at 160°C (320°F). Brush the cold cake with warm apricot jam (sieved), and cover in rolled-out marzipan. For the icing, whisk the egg whites until stiff, gradually whisk in the icing sugar and, when the mixture is stiff, whisk in the glycerine. Using a palette knife spread the icing over the cake.

Christiansfeld honey cake

- 500 g (1 lb) set honey
- 125 g (4 oz) light brown cane sugar
- 1 tsp. ground ginger
- 2 tsp. ground cinnamon
- 3 large eggs, beaten
- 1 tbsp. lowfat plain yoghurt
- 500 g (1 lb) flour
- 2 tsp. bicarbonate of soda

Melt the honey and sugar together then leave to cool. Stir the spices and eggs into the honey/sugar mix, then add the yoghurt and flour with bicarbonate. Pour the cake mix into a greased 28x20 cm (11x8 in) deep baking tin and bake at 160°C (320°C) for approx. 35 minutes. Decorate with scrap pictures or almonds, stuck on with icing.

Ricotta tart

- pre-baked tart case, 22 cm (8¹/2 in) in diam., using ready-made shortcrust pastry (or homemade shortcrust pastry: 250 g (8 oz) flour, 100 g (3¹/2 oz) icing sugar, 125 g (4 oz) butter and 2 pasteurised egg yolks, mixed with 2 tbsp. cold water)
- 100 g (3¹/2 oz) spelt germ (parboiled)
- 250 ml (8 floz) whole milk
- 1 cinnamon stick
- 250 g (8 oz) ricotta
- 2 egg yolks
- 75 g preserved Seville orange peel, finely chopped or ground
- 1 tsp. rosewater
- 75 g sugar
- 2 egg whites
- icing sugar to dust

Boil the spelt germ in milk with the cinnamon stick for 5-20 minutes, until the milk has been absorbed. Cool the porridge and remove cinnamon. Whisk the ricotta with the egg yolks, orange peel, rosewater and sugar. Fold into the porridge. Fold in the whisked egg whites and spread the filling over the pre-baked tart case. Bake at 175°C (340°F), for approx. 45 minutes. Dust with icing sugar.

Chocolate cake

- 2 large eggs
- 90 g (3^1/$_2$ oz) sugar
- 80 g (3^1/$_2$ oz) flour and 1 tsp. baking powder
- 1 tbsp. cocoa powder
- 40 g (1^1/$_2$ oz) butter and 75 g (3 oz) bitter chocolate, melted together

Passion fruit mousse:

- flesh of 4 passion fruits
- 60 g (2^1/$_2$ oz) sugar
- 2 tbsp. orange juice
- 2 egg yolks
- 4^1/$_2$ gelatine leaves, dissolved in 100 ml (3^1/$_2$ floz) warm orange juice
- 150 ml (4^1/$_2$ floz) double cream, whipped

Cream eggs and sugar until thick, add remaining cake ingredients. Bake in 20 cm (8 in) tin for approx. 18 minutes at 175°C (370°F). Heat the passion fruit flesh with the sugar and orange juice. Pass through a sieve. Whisk in the egg yolks, then stir the mixture over a bain marie until thick. Add the dissolved gelatine. Allow the cream to thicken before folding in whipped cream. Split cake in two. Spread cream on one base, then top with second layer. Cut out single portions with a ring cutter, 6 cm (2^1/$_2$ in) in diam.

Twisted doughnuts from South Jutland

- 75 g (3 oz) butter, softened
- 75 g (3 oz) sugar
- grated rind of 1 lemon
- 2 small eggs
- 250 g (8 oz) flour
- 1/2 tsp. bicarbonate of soda
- 2 tbsp. double cream
- oil or vegetable fat for frying
- icing sugar to dust

Cream the butter and sugar, add the other ingredients, and knead to a dough. Leave to rest in a cool place for a couple of hours, before rolling out thinly on baking paper. The long pieces are cut out into finger-wide strips with a pastry wheel, while the rings are cut out with a round cutter. A smaller cutter is used to cut out the hole in the middle. Deep-fry the doughnuts, lay on paper towels to drain, and sift icing sugar on top.

Store the cakes in a cake tin. They will keep for up to a week.

Spanish churros

- 250 ml (8 floz) water
- 75 g (3 oz) butter
- 2 tsp. vanilla sugar
- 125 g (4 oz) flour
- 50 g (2 oz) potato flour
- approx. 5 eggs, beaten
- baking paper
- 1-2 tbsp. butter
- oil for frying

Mix the water, butter and vanilla sugar in a pan. Bring to the boil and add the flour mixed with the potato flour all at once, stirring constantly. Continue to stir until the dough ball comes away from the side of the pan. Turn into a bowl, add a little egg to begin with, and then as much as the dough can absorb. The stirring is hard work, but the finished dough should be smooth, shiny and elastic. Cut out pieces of baking paper and lightly grease them. Place the dough in a piping bag with a large star-shaped nozzle, and pipe a circle on each piece of paper. Heat the oil and hold each piece of paper over the deep-fat fryer until the ring loosens and drops into the oil. Turn the rings with a slotted spoon until they are golden on both sides. Drain on paper towels and sprinkle with more vanilla sugar.

Dutch snowballs

- 10 g (1/2 oz) yeast
- 150 ml (5 floz) milk, tepid
- 1 medium egg
- 200 g (7 oz) flour
- 100 g (31/2 oz) raisins
- oil for frying
- icing sugar to dust

Mix the yeast and milk together, add the egg, flour and raisins, and leave the dough to rise, covered, in a warm place for approx. 1 hour. Using two spoons, shape the dough into small balls and deep-fry them (180°C/350°F) for 2-3 minutes. Drain on paper towels. Serve warm, dusted with icing suger.

Children's baking

Bake honey cookies, dip marshmallows in hot chocolate, bake fun-shaped pepper cookies, or make apple rings and thread them onto a string. Christmas baking comes in many forms, but the most important thing is for children and adults to have fun together. Some of the homemade treats may even last until Christmas!

Classic honey cookies

Makes 10-12 cookies

- 1 jar of honey, 450 g (1 lb)
- 225 g (7¹/2 oz) light brown cane sugar
- 225 g (7¹/2 oz) butter
- 10 g (¹/2 oz) potash
- 2 tbsp. rosewater
- approx. 1 kg (2 lb 2 oz) flour
- 2 tsp. ground cinnamon, 1 tsp. ground ginger and 1 tsp. ground cloves

Bring the honey, sugar and butter to the boil, stirring constantly, and leave to cool. Dissolve the potash in the rosewater, stir the wet ingredients into the tepid honey mixture and add half of the flour, mixed with the spices. Mix well and gradually add the remaining flour. Knead the dough, put it in a plastic bag, and rest in a cool place for 24 hours. Roll out the dough to a thickness of 5mm (¹/2 in), cut into pieces (approx. 9 x 13 cm (3¹/2 x 5 in)), decorate with strips of dough and bake at 200°C (400°F) for 15-18 minutes. Blend 1 egg white with 150 g (5oz) icing sugar and 1 tsp. lemon juice for the icing, and ice the cookies (optional).

Marzipan balls with almonds

- 250 g (8 oz) raw marzipan, grated
- 50 g (2 oz) ground almonds
- 50 g (2 oz) icing sugar
- 1 tbsp. rosewater
- 1 egg for brushing
- 3 whole blanched almonds per ball
- paper baking cases for balls (optional)

Knead the marzipan with the ground almonds, icing sugar and rosewater.

Roll into balls the size of small plums, brush with the egg and press three almonds into the side of each of them. Bake for 10-12 minutes at 175°C (340°F).

57

Spiced pepper cookies

- 100 g (3¹/2 oz) sugar
- 100 ml (3¹/2 fl oz) golden syrup
- 1¹/2 tsp. ground cinnamon
- 1¹/2 tsp. ground ginger
- 1 tsp. ground cloves
- ¹/2 tbsp. bicarbonate of soda
- 100 g (3¹/2 oz) butter
- 1 large/medium egg
- 400 g (14 oz) flour

Bring the sugar, syrup and spices to the boil. Stir in the bicarbonate of soda and pour the mixture over the butter. Stir until the mixture is cold. Add the egg and flour. Knead to a smooth dough – can be used immediately. Roll the dough out thinly on baking paper, cut the cookies out, and bake at 200°C (400°F) for 7-9 minutes.

Send a tube of biscuits

Poster tubes and sweet parcels of crisp, spiced pepper cookies as an edible Christmas greeting are bound to be a hit with the family. The round cookies are cut to a size that perfectly fits the tube. Holes are made in the unbaked cookies with a straw and, once baked, the children can thread a ribbon through so that the cookies can be hung up as decorations. Hearts and stars wait to be sent by the Post Office!

Homemade sweets

Anna and Sofie tasting their produce. They have pushed marshmallows onto long bamboo skewers, dipped them in a cup of melted chocolate and left them to dry on baking paper.

Marzipan hearts

- 250 g (8 oz) raw marzipan, grated
- 50 g (2 oz) ground almonds
- 50 g (2 oz) icing sugar
- 1 tbsp. rosewater
- 1 egg for brushing
- icing as for the honey cookies
- candied peel and cocktail cherries

The recipe for the hearts is the same as for the marzipan balls, so from one portion of dough you can bake two kinds of cake. Knead the marzipan with the almonds, icing sugar and rosewater and roll out to a thickness of 5 mm (1/2 in). Cut out small hearts.

Roll the leftovers into thin sausages and place them around the hearts to form an edge. Brush the edge with the egg and bake for 8-10 minutes at 175°C (340°F). Ice the centre of the heart and decorate with candied peel and cocktail cherries.

Dried apple rings

Another edible gift that can also be used to decorate the Christmas tree. There should be knots in the string to keep the apples apart.

Lay thinly sliced apple rings (core removed) in a cold syrup of 200 ml (7 floz) water, boiled with 200 g (7 floz) sugar and the juice of 1 lemon. Soak for one hour, drain, lay on baking paper on the oven shelf, and dry them at 80°C (150°F) for 4-5 hours. Turn off the oven and leave the apples in there overnight.

Trees and treats

Preparations are a big part of Christmas celebrations.
Making decorations and producing something beautiful from a few
strips of paper, a button and two beads ... that's really quite something!
This chapter is full of ideas for both easy and more challenging things
for the tree, and plenty of ideas that adults and children can enjoy doing
together. A cosy afternoon spent with the family, in the glow of the
Advent candle, can be used to build a sugar castle, or to make fabulous
decorations from wire and beads.

Christmas Eve in Rome in 1833

Tuesday 24 December

In town no one would give us a room as it was such a holy event and we wanted to sing; so we went outside to the big house in the Villa Borghese garden, close to the Amphitheatre by the Pinie wood. Some of us went out there in the morning to set up the party, Jensen and Christensen bound garlands with me; mine was the most tasteful and we decided to give that one to the princess. I laid a festoon of flowers around the table, we had some food there; at three o'clock I went home to do my hair and get dressed. At six o'clock we were all gathered together. Being Catholic, the princess didn't dare come. Plagemann had painted the coats of arms of the three Nordic countries; these hung with oak leaves and laurel garlands between large laurel festoons, I had edged the table with a festoon of flowers and on each plate lay an ivy garland to wear on the head; those for the ladies included roses. We started inside by the Christmas tree, which was a magnificent laurel tree with oranges and presents hanging on it; as luck would have it, I got the best and most expensive present (for 6¹/2 Skudos), a silver beaker with the inscription: "Juleaften i Rom 1833." (Christmas Eve in Rome 1833). And a fine purse as well.

My present, in its many sheets of paper, was the one that brought most joy, being the funniest. Byström got it, and for it I received a round of applause. Hertz received an antique ring, Zeuthen Thorvaldsen's medal given to him by the man himself. At the table, Bøtcher had promised to make much of my song, but he started three tones too high, and refused to admit his mistake, so no one could sing along. This meant that when a toast to the king was proposed, there was a lot of commotion, and the toast was rather flat. Then they were silly enough to sing it once more when the champagne was brought out for the toasts; so the same happened with the toast to the princess: Long live the princess! shouted Blunk. At eleven o'clock, Thorvaldsen and some of the older people left, and I went along with them. As they didn't open the gates when we first knocked, I knocked again. "Chi es?" they asked. "Amice!" we answered and then a little gate was opened, which we crept through. The weather was fine and mild. "Yes," Thorvaldsen said, "it is different from home, my coat is really getting too heavy for me!" Berlin and Carlsberg went wild on us; Fernley talked to Thorvaldsen about seducing me, about my innocence; at the same time the bells were ringing and the people went to Maria Magiora. I went to lie down.

From Hans Christian Andersen's diary.

63

Pastel decorations

Here are plenty of Christmas decorations to get you started:
poinsettia, cones, a fantastic angel for the top of the tree, small
hanging angels and paper rosettes. On these pages, everything
is cut out in delicate pastel shades, but the decorations also look
good in brightly coloured paper.

The Christmas tree and its decorations

A beautifully understated look is created when the entire tree is decorated with homemade decorations in pastel colours. An angel has taken the place of the star at the top of the tree – instructions on how to make it are on the next page.

Poinsettias

You will need:

Handmade 320 g paper, gold foil, gold thread for hanging loops, glue and punch pliers (all from craft shops).

Trace the poinsettia pattern, from the template pages to make template. Draw around the template onto paper. Prick with a needle to show where to cut, and to mark where the holes are to be made. Cut out and make the holes using the smallest setting on the punch pliers. Pinch the tips of each petal to give them form. Cut out 2 small circles (diam. 1.5 cm (1/2 in)) in gold foil. Snip the edges so that the circles become stars. Glue to the centre of the front and back of the flower. Thread gold thread through for hanging.

Tree top angel

You will need: 3 sheets white paper, tape, white handmade tissue paper with silk threads 25 x 60 cm (10 x 24 in), cream handmade tissue paper 30 x 60 cm (12 x 24 in), thick cream paper for the face, gold foil, gold glitter glue, 80 cm (32in) golden satin ribbon 6 mm (^{1}/$_4$ in), 40 cm (16 in) gold wire, a glue stick and a glue gun, black felt tip pen, a stapler and white paper 25 x 60 cm (10 x 24 in) (all available from craft shops).

Dress:

Tape the three sheets of paper together lengthwise, so that they measure 63 cm (25 in) in width. Draw a swirly pattern on the paper in pencil. When you're happy with it, go over in black felt tip. Lay the white tissue paper over the top and make a dotted pattern with glitter glue, following the swirls. Allow to dry, then bunch into an angel dress, hold it flat at the top by fastening with a couple of paperclips.

Wings:

Fold the cream tissue paper widthways, in 1 cm (^{1}/$_2$ in) wide pleats, to form a fan. Bend so that the middle forms a point and the pleats become angel wings. Staple together.

Halo:

Draw and cut out a circle (diam. 6.5 cm (2^1/$_2$ in)) and two circles (diam. 4.5 cm (1^3/$_4$ in)) in gold foil. Make small cuts approx. 1 cm (^{1}/$_2$ in) deep around the edge of the large circle and one of the smaller circles for a fringed effect.

Assembly:

Glue the dress onto the last gold circle with the glue gun. Glue the two fringed circles on top of each other, and glue them to the top of the dress. Wind the wire around the dress to form a hanging loop. Loosely tie the satin ribbon around the neck and allow it to hang down. Glue the angel's body to the pleated wings.

Face:

Trace the angel's face from the template pages at the back of the book, and cut the face out in the thick cream paper. Draw the mouth and eyes with glitter glue. When dry, glue the face into the centre of the fringed halo.

Cones

You will need:

Patterned paper, Mulberry paper (soft and textured) in pastel shades, satin ribbon 6 mm (^{1}/$_4$ in) in pastel shades, double-sided sticky tape 6 mm (^{1}/$_4$ in).

Trace the pattern for the cone, the fringed edge and the handle from the template pages and make card templates. Trace onto patterned paper and cut the pieces out. Trace the fringed edge onto the soft paper and cut out. Snip small fringes along the inside edge. Glue the fringed edge around the top of the cone. Stick a piece of tape on top of the fringed edge approx. 6 mm (^{1}/$_4$ in) from the top edge, leaving the protective strip in place. Stick the cone together. Remove the protective strip from the double-sided sticky tape and press the 70 cm (28 in) satin ribbon into place – tie the ribbon into a bow. Finally glue on the handle.

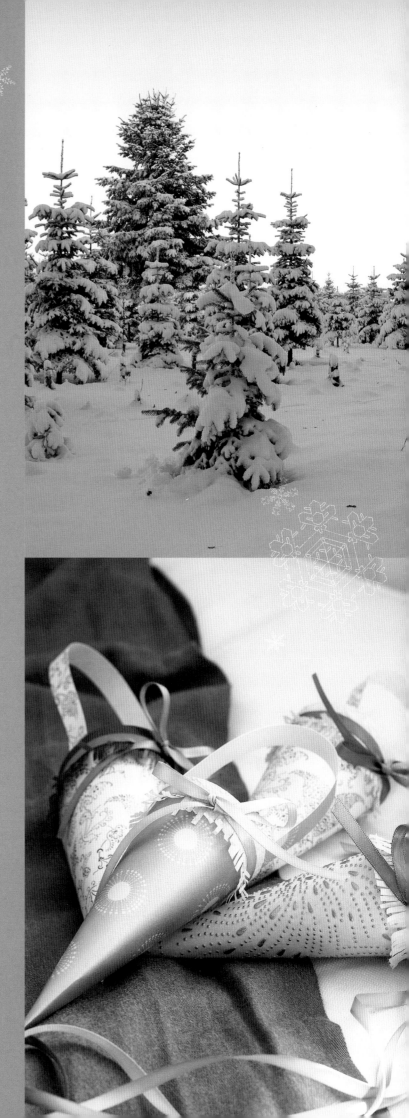

How to make the angels

You will need:

Patterned paper, white Mulberry paper with silk thread, white Canson paper, gold foil, thick card for templates, a glue stick, ruler, scissors, gold thread and double-sided sticky tape.

1. **Trace the template** of the angel's dress from the template pages, onto greaseproof paper with a pencil. Turn the paper over, lay it on the card, and trace over the lines from the back to transfer the pattern. Cut the card template out. Draw around the template on the different papers and cut out.

2. **Fold the angel's dress** and glue it together. Cut out a gold circle with a diameter of 3 cm (1¹/4 in), and snip fringes around the edge. Glue the tip of the dress to the top of the circle. Cut out a circle with a diameter of 1 cm (¹/2 in) from the white Canson paper for the face, and glue on top of the halo and dress.

3. **Cut out a piece** of the white Mulberry paper 10 x 12 cm (4 x 5³/4 in), fold into 1 cm (¹/2 in) wide pleats and pinch in the middle to form a fan on either side. Shape the paper into wings. Glue on a piece of gold thread to make a hanging loop, and glue the angel body to the wings.

Rosette in patterned paper

You will need: Patterned paper, 2 mother-of-pearl buttons, 2 mother-of-pearl beads, gold thread, gold wire, a hole punch and paper clips.

Cut out 10 paper strips of 12 x 1.2 cm (4³/₄ x ¹/₂ in) from patterned paper. Hold them together in a pile with a paper clip. Punch a hole in each end approx. 6 mm (¹/₄ in) from the edge. Thread a bead onto 15 cm (6 in) of wire, and push the ends through one of the buttons and the 2 holes at each end of the paper strips. Remove the paper clip. Stick both ends of the wire through the other button. Then bead. Push 2nd onto one of the ends of the wire, then twist wire together. Spread the paper strips out and attach gold thread for a hanging loop.

Mistletoe leaves and berries

are printed on the mat using a template – it's both easy and fun. The homespun fabric is only 90 cm (36 in) wide, and the white border makes the mat a little larger. Without the border, the mat has a slightly more rustic look.

Christmas tree rug

On Christmas Eve the carpet is hopefully (!) completely covered in presents, but on Christmas Day it will be there for all to see. A Christmas tree rug completes the tree – and if the tree sheds a few needles, it's not the end of the world. The rug is in neutral tones of grey and white, and looks good no matter how colourful your Christmas decorations are.

You will need:

1 m (39 in) homespun grey felt, 90 cm (35 in) wide, 0.5 m (18 in) white, transparent cotton min. 100 cm (36 in) wide, 25 x 35 cm (10 x 14 in) winter white felt, 5 mm (1/4 in) thick, remnants of off-white mohair wool, pinking shears, textile glue, black buttonhole thread, white fabric paint, thick card, a craft knife and brush or sponge.

Using the pinking shears, cut the felt into a 90 x 90 cm (35 x 35 in) square.

How to make the pattern

1. **Trace the motifs,** from the template pages. Transfer the pattern onto the card. Cut out the motif, to make a stencil.

2. **Place the template on the felt.** There should be a large mistletoe branch in each corner and a smaller one between each corner motif. Dab on the paint with a brush or a sponge through the cutout template. When the paint is dry fix by ironing the design (wool setting).

3. **Cut out berries** approx. 1 cm (1/2 in) in diameter. Cut freehand, so they are a little uneven, and you have a mix of large and small berries. Glue berries to the mat with textile adhesive, spreading them out a little. Tie a knot in the buttonhole thread and sew through each berry, attaching at the back so that the berries are firmly in place.

Sewing instructions:

Cut four pieces of the white cotton fabric for the border, according to the measurements on the sketch on the template pages. Machine together at the corners with the fabric inside out. When you reach the point, stop with the needle down, lift the presser foot and turn, lower the presser foot and continue – this ensures a sharp corner. Fold the edges back and press. Place the felt mat on top of the border and pin. Machine sew. Finish with coarse stitching in the white mohair wool over the machine stitching.

A jar full of Christmas spirit

A project for the whole family to create small scenes using all manner of jars.

The jar with the sheep: Fill one third of the jar with sugar. Spread glue onto a branch with small cones, and sprinkle with sugar and glitter. Place the sheep figure on the sugar in the jar.

A ribbon has been tied around the rim of the jar, with two old porcelain pine cones attached to it. A small paper cut-out hangs from the branch.

The jar with the castle: A cheese dome is used to create a colourful nativity scene. Brightly coloured metal foils have been used to make the castle and the figures.

Embellished candle holders

The candle holders are made by twisting and shaping thick, black wire (available from craft shops). Embellish with small droplets of beads and sequins, threaded onto and hung from a small piece of fine florist's wire.

Baby Jesus in a sugar casing

Have a rummage in your Christmas box – you might just find a lovely figure that can be used in the decorative jar. A figure from a nativity scene can certainly lie, or sit in state, in the midst of the sugary landscape. Add a twig dipped in silver glitter for that final touch.

Christmas displays

The key to Christmas decoration in the home is to create small scenes or displays giving a cosy atmosphere to show that Christmas is here. Here are our suggestions for small displays arranged in old and new glasses, cheese domes and jam jars. Everyday sugar becomes an instant winter wonderland – a little imagination never hurt anybody!

Bright colours

*Over the next few pages we show you how to make baskets,
medallions, baubles and stars – all cut out of brightly coloured
card stamped with gold paint. The family will have to help to
make enough decorations for the whole tree!*

Brightly coloured Christmas tree

All card for the decorations has been stamped with gold print, see page 78.
The Christmas mat is made out of a piece of embroidered woollen fabric. We have stamped a gold border around the edge of the mat using fabric paint (from craft shops).

Star on the top of the tree

You will need:

Thick gold wire, gold foil from crafts shops, circle punch (diam. 1.5 cm (3/4 in)) and double-sided sticky tape or glue gun.

Form a thick circle (diam. 4 cm (11/2 in)) from several rounds of wire for the middle of the star. Twist 14 arched lengths of wire (length: 30 cm (12 in) each) in place around the edge of the circle.
Attach a thick spiral of wire (30 cm/12 in) to the bottom of the circle (for fastening to the tree). Twist the 14 arched lengths of wire together in pairs at the tips, to make a seven points then bend into a star shape.
Punch 80 circles out of the gold foil, and glue in pairs on the gold wire.

Christmas baskets

You will need:

Hand-stamped Tukan card, stiff ribbon (70 cm (28 in) per basket), double-sided sticky tape, pattern scissors, punch pliers and a darning needle.

Trace the pattern pieces from the template pages to make card templates. Draw around the templates on the hand-printed card, and cut out the pieces. Cut along the long side of the top piece with the pattern scissors. Score along the dotted lines with the darning needle, and fold and glue the bottom and sides of the box together. Stick double-sided sticky tape along the top edge of the box, and on the back of the 4 sections of the fold-over cuff on the top piece. Fold and glue

the top piece to the outside of the box. Punch holes with the punch pliers, and thread 35 cm (14 in) ribbon through each hole and glue in place. Glue the 2 internal cuffs over the ends of the ribbon to conceal them. Glue the other two internal cuffs in place. Tie the ribbon in a bow.

Christmas medallions

You will need:

Hand stamped Tukan card, thick, textured card, origami or glazed paper, crepe paper, gold foil, gold rickrack ribbon, a glue stick, double-sided sticky tape and compasses (all materials available from craft shops).

Draw 2 circles (diam. 7 cm/2³/4 in) onto thick, textured card and cut them out. Cut a 2 cm (³/4 in) wide strip of crepe paper, and glue to one of the circles, bunching it as you go. Glue a piece of rickrack ribbon to the top of the circle for a hanging loop. Glue the other circle on top. Now for the decoration! Draw and cut out 2 circles (diam. 6.5 cm/2¹/2 in) in glazed or origami paper, and fold into 8 (as making snowflakes). Make small cuts to form a pattern, unfold and, glue onto both sides of the medallion.

Draw circles of different sizes on the hand-printed paper and glue on. Decorate some of the medallions with circles of gold foil, and around the edge.

Christmas baubles

You will need:

Hand-stamped Tukan card with print on both sides, and paperclips.

Cut out 7 circles (diam. 8 cm/3in), and hold them together with 4 paperclips. Mark the centre, and sew the circles together on the sewing machine. Leave a long end of thread to hang to one side. Fold the layers out to form a bauble. Tie a knot in the long ends of thread for the hanging loop.

How to stamp and make stars

You will need:

Brightly-coloured Tukan card, hobby varnish in gold, ornament stamps, small foam roller, double-sided sticky tape, punch pliers and a darning needle (all available from craft shops).

1. **Pour the gold** paint onto a plate and roll onto the stamp. Stamp the patten onto the card and repeat. Use two different stamps and make two quite different papers, using more or less gold print. Some decorations require the print to be on both sides, while others only need it on one side.

2. **Trace the pattern parts** for the star base and the star points from the pattern pages, and make card templates. Cut 16 points out of card with gold print on one side, and mark out the fold lines with the darning needle. Fold the cuffs up.

3. **Draw the star onto the card** with the print on one side and cut out. Glue 8 star points onto one side and then 8 onto the other. Fold the tabs up so that you can clearly see the contrast between the gold printed side and the non-printed side. Punch a hole, and tie a piece of rickrack ribbon through to make a hanging loop.

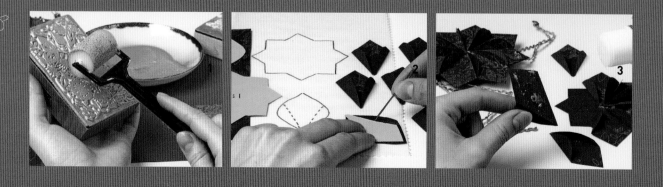

Christmas castle

The children's elf landscape has moved from its humble cave in the forest to more regal surroundings but, never fear, the Christmas spirit has moved with it. Above the magnificent sugar castle is an illuminated heavenly arch where you will find Father Christmas, his sleigh and all his reindeer. The Ultimate Christmas dream!

You will need:

Thick poster tube, metallic paper, granulated sugar and sugar cubes, glue gun, glue stick and craft knife. A metal or wooden tray on which to build the landscape – you will need to drill holes in it! Various figures, a string light and tinsel. Thick wire for the arch over the castle. Glass decorations (optional).

Castle tower:

Glue the metallic paper inside the tube. Cut out a couple of windows and an arched doorway with a hobby knife. The holes should be cut slightly larger than the openings will be when finished. Glue a piece of card covered in gold behind the door opening. Glue on the sugar lumps from the bottom up with the glue gun. Glue both the behind and in between the sugarlumps so that they are firmly in place. The sugar lumps around the door should be cut at an angle to give them a slightly arched shape. Build the tower slightly higher than the cardboard tube, and finish with turrets on the top. Glue glitter around the window openings and here and there on the tower. The glitter will hide any irregularities! Glue on the glass decorations if you are using them.

The tray:

Drill two small holes in the tray so that the wire for the reindeer wreath can be fixed in place. Shape the wire into a circle and wind the string lights around it. Wind the reindeer string around the string lights/wire. The finished circle should be pressed flat at the bottom and attached to the tray by winding thin wire through the holes and the circle. Fill the tray with sugar and allow the children to decorate it with their favourite figures.

Elf in the look-out tower

A little elf keeps watch on the roof of the sugar tower, ready to receive the gifts from Father Christmas when they are dropped from the sleigh. The silver glitter around the windows and here and there on the tower should look like frost and ice flowers.

The fat Christmas goose

The Christmas goose has been fattened up, so the elves at the castle can look forward to Christmas Eve when they might snatch a little roast goose.

Mind the hot glue!

It is a job for an adult to build the actual castle as you will be working with a glue gun – but the decoration can certainly be left to the children's imagination.

Beads for kids

Armed with a roll of soft card wire and plenty of beads and sequins, you can make some really lovely decorations together. Let the kids thread beads and sequins onto the wire and help them to shape crosses, hearts, circles and angels. Hang decorations on the Christmas tree or dot around the house for a festive touch.

Wire decorations with beads

You will need:

Soft card wire, beads with mother-of-pearl finish, small embroidery beads and glass beads, facetted beads, sequins in different shapes and sizes and wire cutters.

Snip a piece of card wire to the required size. Thread beads and sequins onto the wire. Twist the wire around one or two beads to secure the end. Shape into hearts, crosses, circles and angels. For the angel wings, use wire without beads.

Cold, cold Christmas

Let the festive feel start outside – in the window box, on the path, or on the patio. Christmas decorations can be so many things, a few cones and a candle outside, a lantern in the snow or a nicely arranged Christmas sheaf. This section is all about good and simple Christmas ideas, that are both pleasing to the stomachs of the birds in the garden and are a delight to the human eye.

... *In this cold* and in this darkness walked a little girl. She was poor and both her head and feet were bare. Oh, she had had a pair of slippers when she left home; but they had been too big for her - in truth they had belonged to her mother. The little one had lost them while hurrying across the street to get out of the way of two carriages that had been driving awfully fast. One of the slippers she could not find, and the other had been snatched by a boy who, laughingly, shouted that he would use it as a cradle when he had a child of his own.Now the girl walked barefoot through the streets. Her feet were swollen and red from the cold. She was carrying a little bundle of matches in her hand and had more in her apron pocket. No one had bought any all day, or given her as much as a penny. Cold and hungry, she walked through the city, cowed by life, the poor thing! The snowflakes fell on her long yellow hair that curled so prettily at the neck, but to such things she never gave a thought. From every window, of every house, light shone and one could smell the geese roasting all the way out in the street. It was, after all, New Year's Eve; and this she did think about.In a little recess between two houses she sat down and tucked her feet under her. But now she was even colder. She didn't dare go home because she had sold no matches and was frightened that her father would beat her. Besides, her home was almost as cold as the street. She lived in an attic, right under a tile roof. The wind whistled through it, even though they had tried to close the worst of the holes and cracks with straw and old rags. Her little hands were numb from cold. If only she dared strike a match she could warm them a little. She took one and struck it against the brick wall of the house; it lighted! Oh, how warm it was and how clearly it burned like a candle. She held her hand around it. How strange! It seemed that the match had become a big iron stove with brass fixtures. Oh, how blessedly warm it was! She stretched out her legs so that they, too, could get warm, but at that moment the stove disappeared and she was sitting alone with a burned-out match in her hand. She struck another match. Its flame illuminated the wall and it became as transparent as a veil: she could see right into the house. She saw the table spread with a damask cloth and set with the finest porcelain. In the centre, on a dish, lay a roasted goose stuffed with apples and prunes! But what was even more wonderful: the goose - although a fork and knife were stuck in its back - had jumped off the table and was waddling towards her. The little girl stretched out her arms and the match burned out...

Extract from The Little Match Girl by
Hans Christian Andersen. Translated by Erik Haugaard.

Christmas outdoors

How good it feels when the festivities extend beyond the four walls of the house. Here you'll find ideas for outdoor decorations to please both people and birds alike. Simple and easy displays with candles to light on a calm evening, plus birdfood, that you can make in an instant.

Storage in a net

A net of chicken wire is a decorative way to store food while it's waiting to be hung up. The net is made from a 25 x 25 cm (10 x 10 in) piece of chicken wire rolled into a tube. Attach a circle, 8 cm (3 in) in diameter, to form the base of the tube.

Bird cakes in baking tins

It's easy and fun to make birdfood yourself. A basic recipe is on the following page. Pour the mixture into decorative metal cake tins, or roll a small handful into balls and place directly on the bird table.

Clear cold

Oh, how we hope it snows at Christmas! Nothing gives the season a more festive feel than a good coating of white snow. And the children love it!

Lovely berry wreaths

Berries are a real treat for birds in winter. Push dried cranberries onto wire. Twist the ends together and shape into a loop or a hook for hanging. If you are lucky enough to find rowanberries, these are the absolute favourites of winter birds.

Stuffed apples

This is both wet and dry. The core of the juicy apple is replaced with a wild bird mix. Put the food into zinc herb pots, with a little moss around the edges, so that the decoration can be enjoyed by people and birds alike.

Just how the birds like it

- Cracked grains and birdseed mixes are ideal for the bird table, while tallow and seed balls can be hung from the branches of a tree. Apples, pears and rowanberries should be placed on the ground.

- In sub-zero temperatures, it is best to feed the birds with milled seeds (cracked). The birds simply don't have the energy to hack their way through fat and whole seeds.

- Place the birdfood in as stable a position as possible. The food should hang so that the birds can either sit on a branch to eat, or perch on a bird table.

- When it snows, the area should be cleared of snow so that the birds can get to the food.

- Once you have started to put food out for the birds, you should continue throughout the winter.

- Small birds are prey for other animals and they don't feel safe if the bird table is in an open area. Position it close to trees or bushes where the birds can seek quick shelter.

- Place the bird table in front of the kitchen window as it's a pleasure to watch the birds while they eat.

Homemade birdfood

Individual quantities and ingredients may be varied. Mix the ingredients and pour into containers.

500 g (1 lb) melted animal fat, e.g. lard or butter
100 g (3¹/2 oz) sunflower seeds
100 g (3¹/2 oz) ground or blended nuts
100 g (3¹/2 oz) raisins
100 g (3¹/2 oz) porridge oats

Seeds in bottles

Have a rummage around your kitchen for plastic bottles, milk cartons or other "containers". Here we have used a plastic squash bottle, cut down to a height of 4-5 cm (1^1/$_2$ -2 in). Make a hole at the top on both sides and thread a ribbon through. Tie a decorative twig to the ribbon to make the plastic a little more attractive.

Apples on wire

It's easy to push wire through apples. Twist one end around a stick 5-6 times so that the spiral functions as a knot. Then push the apples onto the wire. The hanging apples are intended mainly as decoration as the birds prefer it when apples are left on the ground.

Empty the seed bag
into a granite block

In the summer the granite block with a hole is used for mosquito candles — here in the cold winter months it is both a decorative and solid trough for birdfood. Have a look in the garage to see if you can find any frostproof items normally used in the summer which can take on a new purpose in the winter.

Don't forget the birds

As pretty as it looks to us, it's not easy being a bird in a snow-covered landscape.

Stuffed birchwood

Find a piece of wood in the firewood stack and drill 4-5 range holes. Fill the holes with a fat/seed mix, see previous page. Make a hanger by hammering a hooknail into the top of the wood then tie a thick piece of string through it.

Out with the lanterns

Divine sunshine

In the olden days, angels were often depicted with this special light behind their backs, and it's clear why. The

sun seems divine on a winter's day.

String lights in bell jars

If you have a bell jar, it can be used as a feature on a winter's evening. Switch on a flowery string light, coil it up inside the jar and place it on a tray outside the door. Remember to take it in the same evening as the string light is not intended for outdoor use!

Garden flares in the snow

A lovely display for a calm winter's afternoon and evening. Place a row of garden flares out in the snow and decorate around the candles with small, artificial flowers, pushed well down into the snow.

Lanterns making their winter debut

If you normally use lanterns on balmy summer evenings, why not get them out and let them light up the trees for your Christmas guests. If the lanterns are glass, they will need to be brought in again so that they are not damaged by the snow and frost.

Outside decorations

Decoration for the trees

If you have guests coming in the run up to Christmas, and it is an especially calm afternoon, an outside tree decorated for Christmas cannot fail to delight. The tree needn't be a spruce; any tree or bush with low branches will do. Hang all the decorations close together on a few branches for the best effect.

Pillar candles with wreaths

Find a sheltered spot to stand the tall pillar candles, then decorate them with a few simple twig wreaths wound from fine, pliable twigs from a bush or tree.

A snowy branch

Snowy look for a cold, winter's day.

Thorny wreath with glass birds

Use rambler rose branches to make a wreath. Some ramblers will grow long shoots in the space of one season. Wind the branch into a wreath, using florist wire if necessary to hold it in shape. Decorate with glass birds. It could also be used inside.

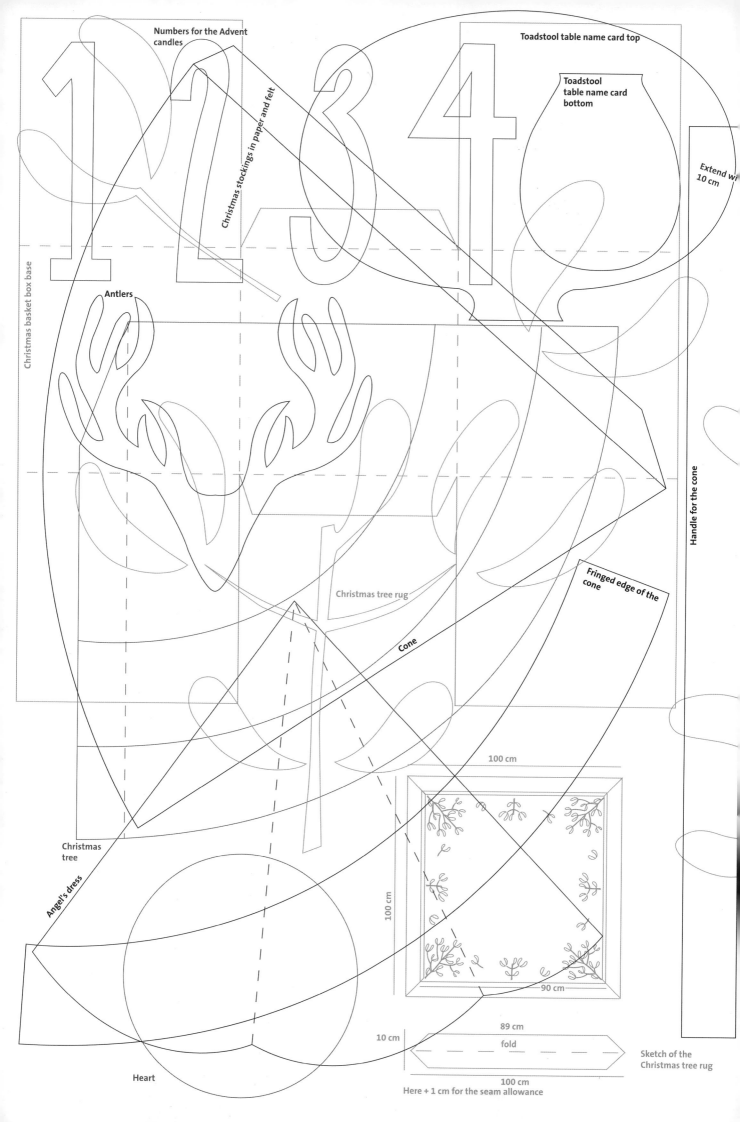

Numbers for the Advent candles

Toadstool table name card top

Toadstool table name card bottom

Christmas stockings in paper and felt

Christmas basket box base

Extend wi 10 cm

Antlers

Handle for the cone

Fringed edge of the cone

Christmas tree rug

Cone

Christmas tree

Angel's dress

100 cm

100 cm

90 cm

Heart

10 cm

89 cm

fold

100 cm

Here + 1 cm for the seam allowance

Sketch of the Christmas tree rug

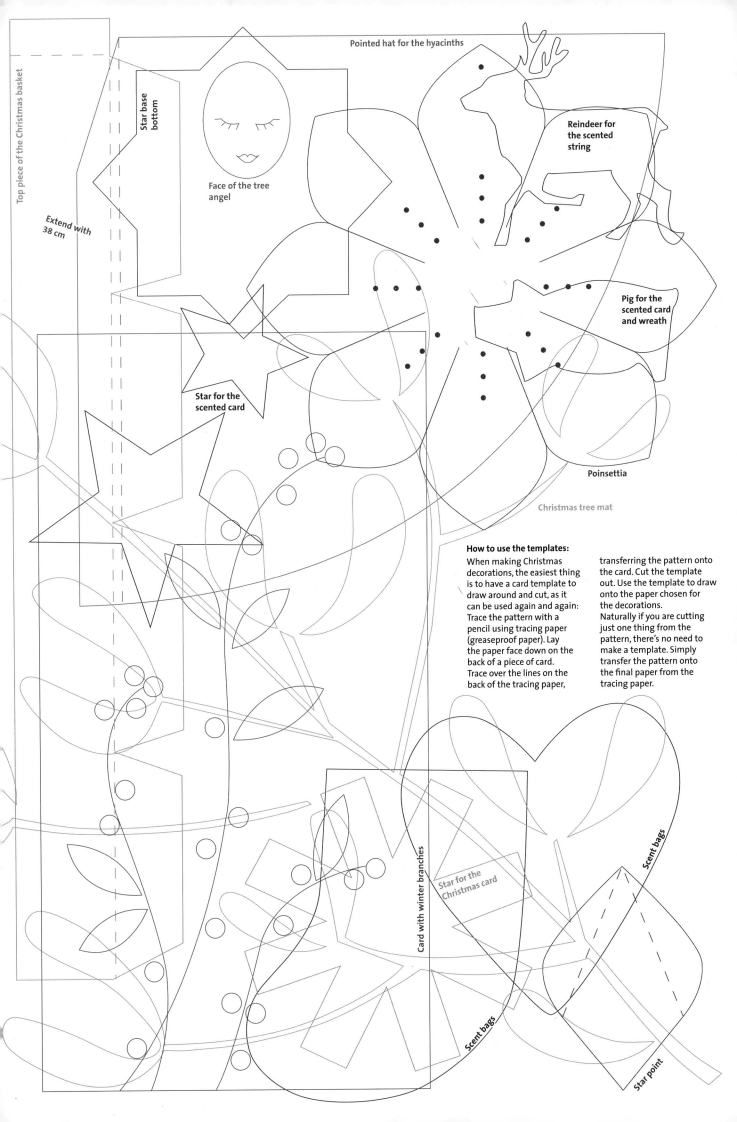

Top piece of the Christmas basket

Extend with
38 cm

Star base
bottom

Pointed hat for the hyacinths

Reindeer for
the scented
string

Face of the tree
angel

Pig for the
scented card
and wreath

Star for the
scented card

Poinsettia

Christmas tree mat

How to use the templates:

When making Christmas decorations, the easiest thing is to have a card template to draw around and cut, as it can be used again and again: Trace the pattern with a pencil using tracing paper (greaseproof paper). Lay the paper face down on the back of a piece of card. Trace over the lines on the back of the tracing paper, transferring the pattern onto the card. Cut the template out. Use the template to draw onto the paper chosen for the decorations.

Naturally if you are cutting just one thing from the pattern, there's no need to make a template. Simply transfer the pattern onto the final paper from the tracing paper.

Card with winter branches

Star for the
Christmas card

Scent bags

Scent bags

Star point